Mapping the World

mapping EUROPE

Gareth Stevens Publishing

By Barbara Linde

Please visit our website, www.garethstevens.com. For a free color catalog of all our high-quality books, call toll free 1-800-542-2595 or fax 1-877-542-2596.

Library of Congress Cataloging-in-Publication Data

Linde, Barbara M.
 Mapping Europe / by Barbara M. Linde.
   p. cm — (Mapping the world)
 Includes index.
 ISBN 978-1-4339-9110-3 (pbk.)
 ISBN 978-1-4339-9111-0 (6-pack)
 ISBN 978-1-4339-9109-7 (library binding)
 1. Europe—Juvenile literature. 2. Europe—Geography—Juvenile literature. I. Linde, Barbara M. II. Title.
 D1051.L56 2014
 940—dc23

First Edition

Published in 2014 by
Gareth Stevens Publishing
111 East 14th Street, Suite 349
New York, NY 10003

Copyright © 2014 Gareth Stevens Publishing

Designer: Katelyn E. Reynolds
Editor: Kristen Rajczak

Photo credits: Cover, p. 1 (photo) Vitaly Titov & Maria Sidelnikova/Shutterstock.com; cover, p. 1 (map) Alexrk2/Wikipedia.com; cover, pp. 1–24 (banner) kanate/Shutterstock.com; cover, pp. 1–24 (series elements and cork background) iStockphoto/Thinkstock.com; p. 5 Vitoriano Junior/Shutterstock.com; pp. 5 (compass rose), 7, 9 (inset) iStockphoto/Thinkstock.com; 9 (main) The World Factbook/CIA; p. 11 (inset) Gena96/Shutterstock.com; p. 11 (main) silver tiger/Shutterstock.com; p. 13 (inset) AridOcean/Shutterstock.com; p. 13 (main) Dan Breckwoldt/Shutterstock.com; p. 15 (inset) Dmitry Naumov/Shutterstock.com; p. 15 (main) LiliGraphie/Shutterstock.com; p. 17 (inset) pavalena/Shutterstock.com; p. 17 (main) Patricia Hamilton/FlickrVision/Getty Images; p. 19 (inset) Neftali/Shutterstock.com; p. 19 (main) Samot/Shutterstock.com; p. 20 (Parthenon sketch) Danussa/Shutterstock.com; p. 21 (flag Vjom/Shutterstock.com; p. 21 (flags) Hemera/Thinkstock.com; p. 21 (map) dalmingo/Shutterstock.com.

All rights reserved. No part of this book may be reproduced in any form without permission in writing from the publisher, except by a reviewer.

Printed in the United States of America

CPSIA compliance information: Batch #CS13GS: For further information contact Gareth Stevens, New York, New York at 1-800-542-2595.

CONTENTS

Welcome to Europe 4

Where Is Europe? 6

The Countries of Europe 8

Joining Together 10

Oceanside to Mountainside 12

Europe's Climates 14

The Resources of Europe 16

Europe's Crowded Streets 18

The Landmarks of Europe 20

Glossary 22

For More Information 23

Index 24

Words in the glossary appear in **bold** type the first time they are used in the text.

WELCOME TO EUROPE

Look at the **continent** of Europe on the map on the next page. The Arctic Ocean lies to the north. The Mediterranean Sea and the continent of Africa lie to the south. The Atlantic Ocean is to the west. To the east, the Ural Mountains form the border that separates Europe from the continent of Asia. Use the **compass rose** on the map on page 5 to help you find these **boundaries**.

Many large and small islands are part of Europe. Several **archipelagos** are, too.

Where in the World?

Some people think the continent was named after Europa, a woman in ancient Greek stories. Others think it's a word from an ancient language meaning "where the sun set."

WHERE IS EUROPE?

Latitude and **longitude** can help us find any place on Earth. Latitude lines run east and west above and below the equator. The equator divides Earth into two halves, or hemispheres. Above the equator is the Northern Hemisphere, and below the equator is the Southern Hemisphere.

Longitude lines run north and south on either side of the Prime Meridian. The Prime Meridian divides Earth into Eastern and Western Hemispheres.

Europe is in the Northern Hemisphere. It's mostly in the Eastern Hemisphere.

Where in the World?

Latitude and longitude lines are measured in degrees. The equator and Prime Meridian are both at 0°.

Using the measurements of latitude and longitude, called coordinates, you would be able to find any city in Europe!

Prime Meridian

7

THE COUNTRIES OF EUROPE

Europe is divided into more than 40 countries. You may have heard of countries like Italy, France, Germany, and Spain. Estonia, Belarus, Poland, and Belgium are also European countries.

Russia is the largest country in Europe—and in the world! It has an area of more than 6.5 million square miles (17 million sq km). With an area of only 0.17 square mile (0.44 sq km), Vatican City is the smallest country. It's actually inside the country of Italy!

Where in the World?

Several famous children's authors are from Europe. J. K. Rowling, author of the Harry Potter series, was born in England. Jacob and Wilhelm Grimm, who wrote books of fairy tales, were from Germany.

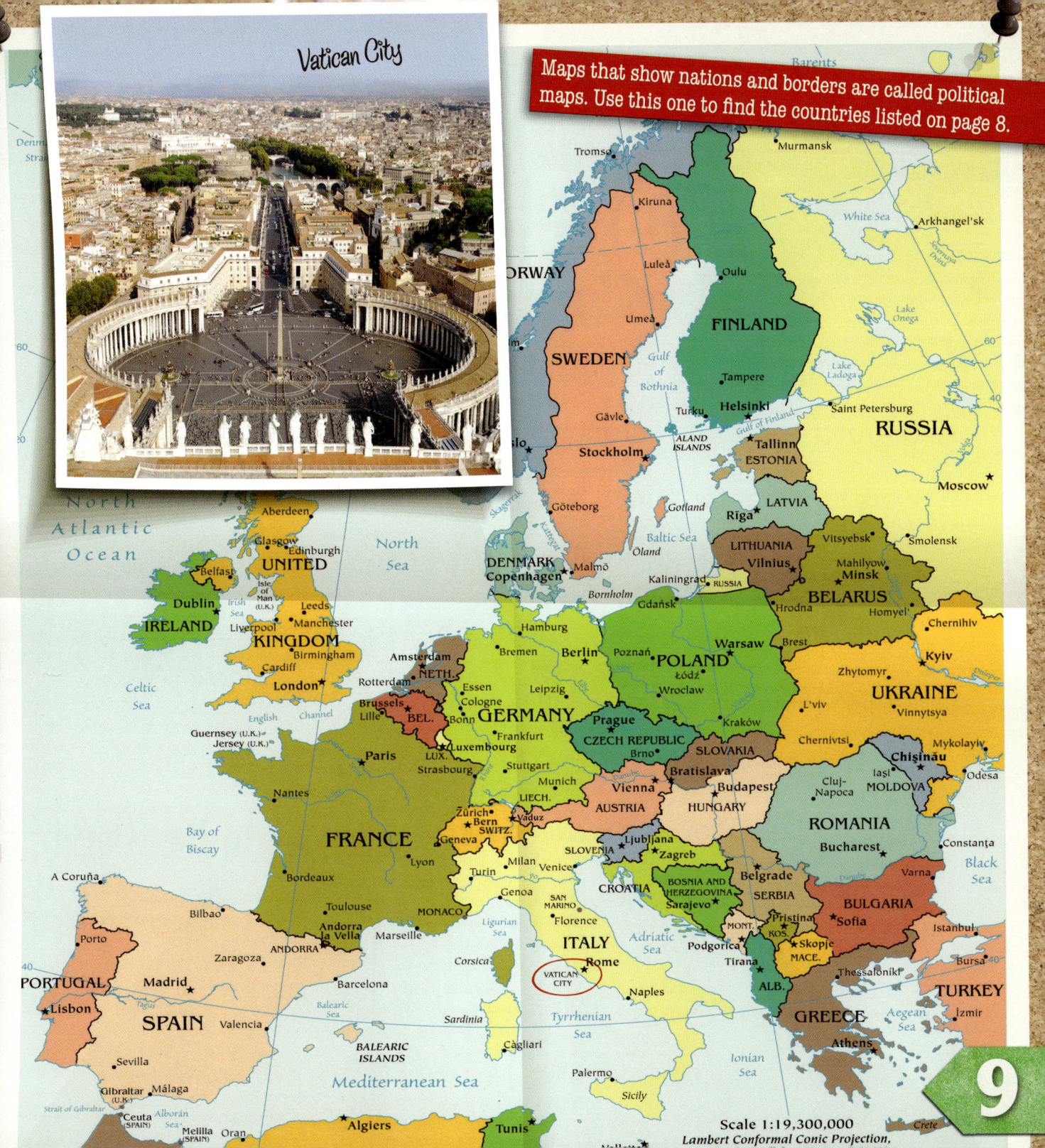

9

JOINING TOGETHER

Since 1993, 27 European countries have become part of a group called the European Union, or EU. These countries work together for peace and equality. The EU countries trade goods with each other. Many of the member countries share one kind of money, called the euro. This makes it easy for people to buy and sell things in all the countries.

People who live in an EU country can easily visit other EU countries. They can move to the different countries for work, too.

Where in the World?

Belgium, France, Germany, Italy, Luxembourg, and the Netherlands took the first step toward the EU in 1951. They formed a group called the European Coal and Steel Community.

OCEANSIDE TO MOUNTAINSIDE

Will you find landforms such as mountains, valleys, and rivers in Europe? You bet!

A mountain range called the Alps is about 750 miles (1,200 km) long. It crosses France, Italy, Switzerland, and other European countries. The longest river in Europe, the Volga River, flows through much of Russia. Low grasslands make up the Great Hungarian Plain. In Norway and Greenland, **fjords** (fee-OHRDZ) reach inland. The Meseta is a high **plateau** in Spain. A few small deserts dot Europe, too.

Where in the World?

The English Channel is a narrow body of water that separates England and France. A long tunnel, called the Chunnel, runs under the channel and connects the two countries. Trains run through it!

Relief maps, such as the one of Europe on the left, show the landforms, plant growth, and other natural features of an area. The beautiful Alps in the picture below would commonly be shown on a relief map.

13

EUROPE'S CLIMATES

Europe has many different **climates**. Do you like cold weather? Greenland, Iceland, and northern Russia are just the places for you. If you don't mind a lot of quick changes to the weather, go to Slovakia or the Czech Republic. Visit Greece to enjoy a hot, dry summer.

Spend some time in the United Kingdom (England, Scotland, Wales, and Northern Ireland) if you welcome a lot of rain. Estonia and Latvia both have warm, dry summers and cold, snowy winters.

Where in the World?

Since records began officially being kept in 1956, the coldest temperature in Europe was on December 31, 1978, in Ust'-Schugor, Russia. It was −72.6°F (−58.1°C). Athens, Greece, reached the highest temperature of 118.4°F (48.0°C) on October 7, 1977.

French Alps

People enjoy the warm, sunny beaches along the Mediterranean Sea in France and Italy. This area is often called the Riviera.

15

THE RESOURCES OF EUROPE

Europe's **natural resources** include coal, iron, silver, and gold. Some oil and natural gas comes from under the North Sea. Russia is one of the largest producers of oil and natural gas in the world.

Because there are so many **peninsulas** and islands, most countries in Europe aren't very far away from an ocean. Fishing is a big industry in many nations, including Norway, Iceland, and Russia. Some of the continent's many rivers are used to make electricity, too.

Where in the World?
Farmers in Europe are some of the greatest producers of potatoes, oats, and wheat.

The village of Alnes, Norway, has a lovely harbor full of fishing boats. Alnes is most famous for its lighthouse, which you can see in the background of this picture.

EUROPE'S CROWDED STREETS

Most Europeans live in cities. Many cities—such as Rome, Italy, and Athens, Greece—are very old. You can see ancient ruins close to new, modern buildings. The cities often have narrow, winding streets. There are many outdoor markets and parks. People use trains, bikes, or cars to get around—or they walk!

One of the largest cities in Europe is Moscow, Russia. About 11.5 million people live there! Around 8 million people live in London, England.

Where in the World?

The city of St. David's, UK, has only about 2,000 residents. Hum, Croatia, may be the smallest town in Europe. Only about 20 people live there.

Those who live in London, England, might use a map like the one below to get around the Underground, or the "Tube." Or, they might ride on London's famous double-decker buses!

map of the Underground

19

THE LANDMARKS OF EUROPE

Every continent has special places called landmarks. People build landmarks to remember a person, to celebrate an event, or to use for a special purpose. The Leaning Tower of Pisa in Italy, for example, was built to be a bell tower!

One of the most famous landmarks in Europe is Stonehenge, an ancient ring of huge stones in England. The Acropolis in Athens, Greece, was built thousands of years ago. Parts of the Acropolis's temples and other buildings are still standing.

Parthenon on the Athenian Acropolis

Where in the World?

Several bridges, all called the London Bridge, have been built in the same place in London for thousands of years. The nursery rhyme, "London Bridge Is Falling Down," was written about this famous landmark.

GLOSSARY

archipelago: a group of islands

boundary: the line, fence, landform, or other object that separates one country from another

climate: the average weather conditions of a place over a period of time

compass rose: a map symbol that shows the four cardinal directions: north, south, east, and west

continent: one of the seven large landmasses on Earth. They are Asia, Europe, Africa, North America, South America, Australia, and Antarctica.

fjord: a long, narrow inlet of the ocean between high cliffs

latitude: the imaginary lines that run east and west above and below the equator

longitude: the imaginary lines that run north and south on either side of the Prime Meridian

natural resource: something in nature that can be used by people

peninsula: a piece of land that sticks out from a larger landmass and is almost completely surrounded by water

plateau: an area of level ground that is higher than the ground around it

FOR MORE INFORMATION

Books

Gibson, Karen Bush. *Spotlight on Europe*. Mankato, MN: Capstone Press, 2011.

National Geographic. *National Geographic World Atlas for Young Explorers*. Washington, DC: National Geographic Society, 2010.

Newman, Sandra. *Europe*. New York, NY: Children's Press, 2009.

Websites

Europa Kids' Corner
europa.eu/kids-corner/index_en.htm
Read facts about the European Union. Play games and take quizzes to check your understanding.

Europe: Geography
www.ducksters.com/geography/europe.php
Use this website to learn more about the geography, history, and culture of Europe. View detailed maps of Europe.

Publisher's note to educators and parents: Our editors have carefully reviewed these websites to ensure that they are suitable for students. Many websites change frequently, however, and we cannot guarantee that a site's future contents will continue to meet our high standards of quality and educational value. Be advised that students should be closely supervised whenever they access the Internet.

INDEX

Alps 12, 13, 15
Athens, Greece 14, 18, 20
Belgium 8, 10
boundaries 4
cities 18
climates 14
compass rose 4, 5
countries 8, 9, 10, 11, 12
England 8, 12, 14, 18, 19, 20
English Channel 12
equator 6
European Union (EU) 10, 11
France 8, 10, 12, 15
Germany 8, 10
Great Hungarian Plain 12
Greece 4, 14, 18
hemispheres 6
Italy 8, 10, 12, 15, 18, 20
landforms 12, 13
landmarks 20
latitude 6, 7
London, England 18, 19, 20
longitude 6, 7
Mediterranean Sea 4, 15
Meseta 12
Moscow, Russia 18
natural resources 16
North Sea 16
Norway 12, 16, 17
political maps 9
Prime Meridian 6, 7
relief maps 13
Riviera 15
Rome, Italy 18
Russia 8, 12, 14, 16, 18
Spain 8, 12
Ural Mountains 4, 5
Volga River 12